PERCY LAVON
JULIAN

PIONEERING CHEMIST

PERCY LAVON

JULIAN

PIONEERING CHEMIST

by Darlene R. Stille

Content Adviser: Ben Keppel, Ph.D.,
Associate Professor of History,
University of Oklahoma

Reading Adviser: Alexa L. Sandmann, Ed.D.,
Professor of Literacy, College and Graduate School
of Education, Health, and Human Services,
Kent State University

Compass Point Books ✦ Minneapolis, Minnesota

Compass Point Books
151 Good Counsel Drive
P.O. Box 669
Mankato, MN 56002-0669

Editor: Anthony Wacholtz
Page Production: Bobbie Nuytten
Photo Researcher: Eric Gohl
Cartographer: XNR Productions, Inc.
Library Consultant: Kathleen Baxter

Art Director: LuAnn Ascheman-Adams
Creative Director: Joe Ewest
Editorial Director: Nick Healy
Managing Editor: Catherine Neitge

Library of Congress Cataloging-in-Publication Data
Stille, Darlene R.
  Percy Lavon Julian : pioneering chemist / by Darlene R. Stille.
      p. cm.—(Signature Lives)
  Includes bibliographical references and index.
  ISBN 978-0-7565-4089-0 (library binding)
1. Julian, Percy Lavon, 1899–1975—Juvenile literature. 2. Chemists—
United States—Biography—Juvenile literature. 3. African American
chemists—Biography—Juvenile literature. I. Title.
  QD22.J75S86 2009
  540.92—dc22   2008038462

Visit Compass Point Books on the Internet at *www.compasspointbooks.com*
or e-mail your request to *custserv@compasspointbooks.com*

MODERN AMERICA

Life in the United States since the late 19th century has undergone incredible changes. Advancements in technology and in society itself have transformed the lives of Americans. As they adjusted to this modern era, people cast aside old ways and embraced new ideas. The once silenced members of society—women, minorities, and young people—made their voices heard. Modern Americans survived wars, economic depression, protests, and scandals to emerge strong and ready to face whatever the future holds.

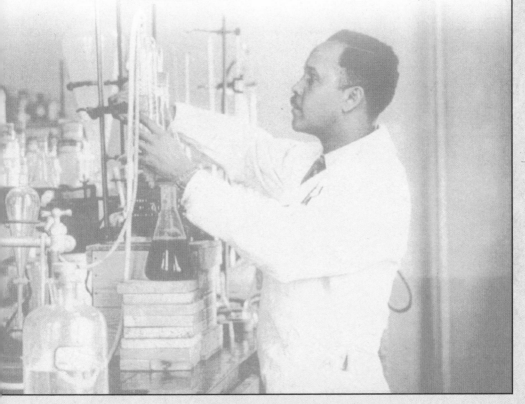

Table of Contents

Chapter

1 TAKE HEART

❦

In 1935, Percy Lavon Julian took a risky chance. He was a young, unknown African-American chemist. Yet he dared to challenge the work of a great British chemist, one of the best-known chemists in the world. Both scientists were trying to create a drug to treat glaucoma, a serious eye disease that can cause blindness. Julian dared to tell the British chemist that his way of going about this task was wrong.

He published his challenge in a journal that was read by chemists all over the world. Many of Julian's friends and co-workers feared that the young chemist had ruined his career. If Julian were wrong, he might never again be hired to do any kind of research.

Julian turned out to be right. He found a way to

Percy Julian was one of the most successful African-American chemists in U.S. history.

Scientists have found many powerful chemicals in plants that can be made into drugs. Some of these drugs cure diseases, such as malaria and even some forms of cancer. However, one of the most common drugs originally made from a plant is aspirin. Aspirin can relieve aches and pains and bring down fevers. In the 1800s, chemists found that salicin, a substance in willow bark, was a pain reliever. German chemists later learned how to synthesize salicinlike substances called salicylic and acetylsalicylic acids. In 1899, the Bayer Company in Germany began to sell the pain-relieving compounds as aspirin.

make an affordable drug for treating glaucoma. The drug came from a bean that grew in Africa. It was the first of many discoveries made by Julian.

Like other chemists in the early and mid-1900s, Julian was breaking ground in a new science called natural products chemistry. He was learning how to unlock the secrets of drugs found in plants. He was also learning to re-create these natural drugs in the laboratory. The drugs he was able to create were much less expensive than the drugs taken from the plants.

It is not suprising that Julian became a plant chemist. From the time he was a young boy, he was fascinated by plants. He began to learn about plants by taking walks in the woods and fields near his home in Alabama. He began to learn about science by reading books in his father's library.

Julian especially liked reading about chemistry. He wanted to know about all the various

substances the world is made of. He wanted to
know how one substance combined with another.
He wanted to know how these substances changed.
He especially wanted to study the chemicals that
plants made.

*Julian used
many tools and
equipment in
his laboratory
to study various
substances and
chemicals.*

Thinking back to his childhood days, he said:

> *How wonderful the plant laboratory seems.*
> *... There is never any end to the story. I*
> *remember as a boy of 17 years of age, this*
> *was a fascinating thing for me: how we*
> *human beings breathe out carbon dioxide*
> *into the air, the leaves of plants pick this*
> *carbon dioxide up, and the plant gives off*
> *oxygen, which we can breathe in and keep*
> *our life going.*

Julian wanted to become a chemist when he grew up. Before he could fulfill his dream, however, he had many obstacles to overcome. He was an African-American growing up in the South in the early 1900s. African-Americans faced racial discrimination and prejudice in every area of life. There were few opportunities for black children to attend school.

Julian, however, managed to get a good education with the support of his family and friends. He traveled north to Indiana and earned a bachelor's degree from DePauw University. With the help of a scholarship, he earned a master's degree from Harvard University. He then went on to earn a doctorate in chemistry in Austria.

After graduating, however, he found that there were few job opportunities for black chemists. Julian was determined to make his mark in science, and

that was why he took the chance of challenging the work of the British chemist.

Julian should have had many job offers after creating the drug to treat glaucoma. In the 1930s, however, no U.S. university would hire an African-American as a professor to teach white students. Most schools, including colleges and universities, were racially segregated or allowed only a few black students. So, despite several great accomplishments, Julian had no chance of being hired as a professor at

African-Americans were forced to use separate drinking fountains in the South.

a white school. At that time, there were also few jobs for black chemists in industry.

But an executive at the Glidden Paint Company recognized Julian's brilliance and talent. The executive hired him as the first African-American to head a research laboratory for a major company. In this job, Julian looked for substances that could be made from soybeans. From his laboratory came coatings for paper, water-based paint, salad dressings, margarine, dog food, and most importantly, medicines.

Because of his discoveries, Julian came to be recognized as one of the greatest natural-product chemists of the 1900s. He founded his own company, Julian Laboratories, and helped other African-Americans begin their careers as chemists. He also worked with organizations to help African-Americans win equal opportunities in housing, jobs, and education. He was given many awards and honorary degrees.

Julian faced incredible hardships on his journey to greatness as a scientist. But he never gave up. Looking back on his life, Julian remembered a line from a poem by Donald Adams that had inspired him: "Take heart, I told myself, Go farther on." During troubled times later in life, Julian said:

> *My dear friends, who daily climb uncertain hills in the countries of their minds,*

hills that have to do with the future of our country and of our children, may I humbly submit to you, the only thing that has enabled me to keep doing the creative work, was the constant determination: Take heart! Go farther on! ❧

With his wife Anna at his side, Julian (center) received the first McNaughton Medal for Public Service in 1972.

2 LIFE IN THE SOUTH

Chapter

❧❀❧

Percy Julian's success as a scientist was unusual for an African-American during the early 1900s, especially in the South. He was born April 11, 1899, "at the corner of Jeff Davis Avenue and South Oak Street in Montgomery, Alabama—the Capital in the cradle of the confederacy." More than half a century later, Montgomery became a cradle of the modern civil rights movement. It was here that the Reverend Martin Luther King Jr. led a boycott to end racial segregation of buses in Montgomery. The protest had been sparked in 1955 by a black seamstress, Rosa Parks, who was arrested for refusing to give up her bus seat to a white man.

When he was growing up in the early 1900s, laws denying basic civil rights made life hard for Percy and

Martin Luther King Jr. advocated for civil rights and the end of segregation.

other African-Americans. These so-called Jim Crow laws kept African-Americans segregated from white Southerners in many ways. For example, if Percy and his playmates grew thirsty on a hot summer day in Montgomery, they had to drink from a fountain for "coloreds" only. African-Americans could not stay in "white" hotels or eat in "white" restaurants. Those lucky enough to have money for the movies had to sit in a "coloreds-only" theater.

White Southerners in the 1800s used a stage character named Jim Crow to make racial slurs against African-Americans. Whites in "blackface" makeup played the Jim Crow character, dancing and singing silly songs to depict blacks as foolish and ignorant.

The Jim Crow laws made it almost impossible for African-Americans to vote and prevented black students from getting a good education. Schools were strictly segregated, with black and white students going to different schools. The black schools did not have good textbooks and other supplies found in schools for whites. There were no public high schools for African-American students. For most black teenagers, education stopped at the eighth grade.

The divisions between blacks and whites were severe in Alabama. Their situation grew worse, however, when Percy was 2 years old. In 1901, Alabama adopted a new state constitution. Wealthy

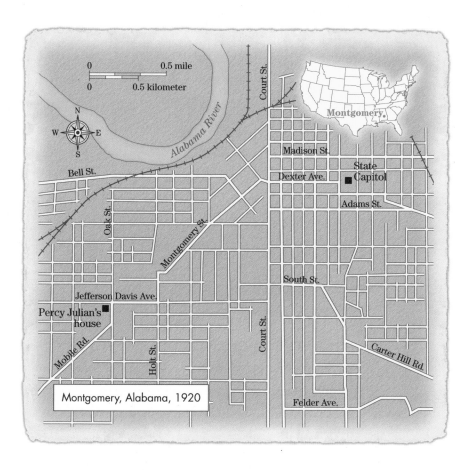

Montgomery, Alabama, 1920

white men designed Alabama's 1901 constitution to wipe out voting rights and other rights granted to African-Americans after the Civil War.

Before the Civil War—which was fought from 1861 to 1865—slavery was legal in Alabama and other Southern states. In fact, Percy's grandparents had been enslaved on a plantation. Slavery ended with President Abraham Lincoln's Emancipation Proclamation and the defeat of the South.

Montgomery, Alabama, was a site of segregation and discrimination during Percy's childhood.

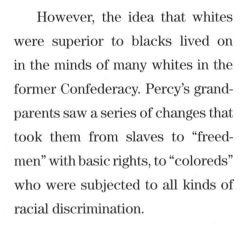

In February 1861, the Confederate States of America was established, with Montgomery as its first capital. In May, Richmond, Virginia, became the new capital, but Montgomery was called the cradle of the confederacy.

However, the idea that whites were superior to blacks lived on in the minds of many whites in the former Confederacy. Percy's grand-parents saw a series of changes that took them from slaves to "freed-men" with basic rights, to "coloreds" who were subjected to all kinds of racial discrimination.

The series of changes began right after the Civil War, during a period called Reconstruction. Its purpose was to readmit Alabama and 10 other Southern states to the Union, build roads and railroads, and feed starving blacks and whites living in poverty in the war-ravaged region. The federal government also wanted former slaves, now called freedmen, to be treated fairly.

Union soldiers occupied the former Confederate territory. Freedmen, Northerners, and Alabamans who supported the goals of the Union joined together in the Republican Party, the party of Abraham Lincoln. They took over the state's government. Black Alabamans were elected to public office, including to the U.S. Congress. Before the Civil War, it had been illegal for slaves to learn how to read and write. During Reconstruction, schools were set up for black children, who went on to

become teachers of other black children.

The U.S. Constitution was amended to make slavery unconstitutional (under the 13th Amendment) and extend basic citizenship rights to African-Americans. The 14th Amendment guaranteed equal protection under the law to everyone. The 15th Amendment granted African-American men the right to vote.

The situation for black Alabamans took a turn for the worse in 1874. Reconstruction ended, and the Union soldiers went home. White landowners, merchants, and other wealthy white men in Alabama's

African-American children in the South learned harvesting practices in school.

Democratic Party took back control of the state government. They used violence and voting fraud to win elections. To be sure that they would hold on to power, they proposed the 1901 constitution. It set up many rules and restrictions that made it almost impossible for black men and many poor white men to vote. (Women were not yet allowed to vote.)

To persuade others to adopt the new constitution, the Democrats had a slogan: "White Supremacy, Honest Elections and the New Constitution, One and Inseparable." Future elections would be "honest" because the white, conservative Democrats would no longer have to steal the vote, they said. They made sure that people who opposed them could not vote.

White hate groups such as the Ku Klux Klan threatened, attacked, and even killed blacks, and did the same to white people who objected to the unfair treatment of African-Americans. Many African-Americans were lynched. Drinking from a whites-only fountain or any act that whites thought of as insulting could lead to a violent death.

Born into this dangerous world of segregation and discrimination, young Percy depended on his family for love and support. Percy, his two brothers, and his three sisters were fortunate. Both of their parents had gone to a school for black students. Percy's mother, Elizabeth, was a teacher. She taught Percy to read and do math when he was a young boy,

Ku Klux Klan members demonstrated during a parade in Washington, D.C. The racist group ran a violent campaign of terror.

and she often took him to school with her. Because of his mother, young Percy learned to love great works of literature, especially novels and poetry.

Percy's father, James, had a good job as a railway mail clerk. Before becoming a mail clerk, James Julian had been a teacher and a principal

Elizabeth Julian

in a school for black children. He loved books and learning. He was interested in many things, including science and math. He bought what books he could to build a library for his children. African-American children were not allowed into public libraries in the South. By reading his father's science books, Percy became fascinated with chemistry.

The books introduced him to the world of chemical elements. He read that the smallest unit of a chemical element is an atom, which is much too small to see. He learned that various kinds of atoms join together to make molecules. He also learned that two hydrogen atoms and one oxygen atom make up a molecule of water. He discovered that carbon and oxygen atoms join to create molecules of carbon dioxide, the gas his lungs gave off when he exhaled.

Julian realized that every substance in the world is made of molecules. Some substances are complex. They contain atoms of many other chemical elements, such as nitrogen, chlorine, and iron.

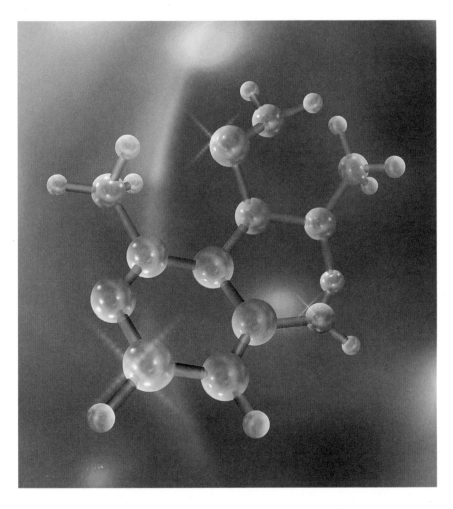

The molecules of some substances are complex and contain many atoms.

Percy did not learn just from books. He also learned when he walked in the nearby woods with his father on Sunday afternoons. His father talked with him about the native plants they saw growing around Montgomery. Percy began to realize that the plants also produced chemicals and wondered what the chemicals were. Little did he know that he was beginning to think about the next chemical frontier. He was thinking about what would come to be called natural products chemistry. Walking, talking, and thinking on those outings with his father was an experience that Julian never forgot. He later recalled:

> *Every time I have tackled a new natural product ... the memory of the Sunday afternoon walks through the woods and field has remained with me.*

Percy was also close to his grandparents, Cabe and Livonia Julian. He loved to visit them on their farm during the summer to help plant, pull weeds, and harvest cotton. Looking at his grandfather's hard-working hands was a reminder of how precious an education can be. One hand had only three fingers. While a slave, Cabe had committed the "crime" of learning to read and write. As punishment, his owner ordered that two of his fingers be cut off.

Percy always remembered his grandfather for the wisdom he taught. "My children and my friends all know him as Grandpa Cabe," recalled Julian "because they've heard me speak about him so many times." One day Percy and his brother James were working alongside others in the cotton field. "We were singing on that day a beautiful spiritual, 'There is a balm in Gilead to make the wounded whole. There is a balm in Gilead to heal the sin-sick soul.'

'Grandpa Cabe,' I asked, 'what's a balm in Gilead?'

'Well, Sonny, you see, Gilead was a famous town in Israel for the manufacture of salves to heal wounds and sores,' he told me. 'And they called these salves balms.'"

Julian learned a new word, but his grandfather went on with this story from the Bible to teach him a new way of looking at life. The Christian church was a powerful force in the lives of African-Americans. Their faith helped slaves and former slaves get through many hardships. African-Americans drew lessons for

Many African-American families in the early 1900s spent much of their day in the fields picking cotton by hand.

Jeremiah was an Old Testament prophet who proclaimed that people should repent of their evil ways.

their own lives from the stories in the Bible.

On that day, Grandpa Cabe used the story of the ancient Israelite leader Jeremiah to teach Julian a lesson that always stuck with him:

Now one day Jeremiah was having a hard time trying to lead his people the right way. Everything was going wrong for Jeremiah, and he cried out in anguish, "Is there no balm in Gilead?" You see, what he was saying was, "Ain't there no way out?" I want you to know that, Sonny, because I believe there is always a way out.

Percy later recalled, "It was then that I made my vow—that I would forever fight to keep hope alive because there is always a way out."

Like many African-Americans, Julian and his family believed that the way out of a life of poverty and discrimination was through education. Percy's mother and father wanted all their children to have a college education. Percy was the first of his brothers and sisters to go to college. With the help of his family, he was ready to fight to keep the hope of education alive.

3 A Thirst for Learning

 ☙⌘❧

One autumn day in 1916, Percy Julian dressed in his best suit and tie and said farewell to his family. His grandparents, parents, brothers, and sisters went to the train station to see him off. He boarded a train for Greencastle in the Northern state of Indiana, ready for new experiences as a student at DePauw University.

In those days, DePauw University was a small liberal arts college that had admitted a few African-American students since the Civil War. Soon after the train pulled into the Greencastle station, Julian realized that he had not left racial discrimination behind. There was plenty of it in the North as well. He learned that he was the only black student enrolled at DePauw. He was told that he could not live in a college dormitory because of the color of

St. Elmo Brady became a role model for African-Americans who wanted to further their education at a college or university.

his skin. Instead, he was taken to a boarding house off campus. He was hungry after his journey, but the white woman who ran the boarding house told him that she would not serve him any meals. He had to walk around town looking for a restaurant that would serve an African-American.

His first days in Greencastle were a confusing time for Julian. Some people treated him with the same disrespect he had experienced in Montgomery. Others were more open to having an African-American classmate. He recalled:

One of the first and most famous black schools was the Tuskegee Institute in Alabama. It was headed by the famous black educator Booker T. Washington, who was born into slavery. The institute taught African-Americans practical skills such as how to become teachers, farmers, and blacksmiths. In 1985, the school became Tuskegee University.

> *On my first day in college, I remember walking in and a white fellow stuck out his hand and said, "How are you?—Welcome!" I had never shaken hands with a white boy before and did not know whether I should or not.*

His college experience was about to make him feel even more like an outsider. Julian's earlier education in Montgomery had put him at a great disadvantage. He could not enroll as a regular college freshman. Instead, he had to enroll as a "subfreshman." He was not prepared for college courses. Because there were no high schools in Alabama for African-Americans, Julian had attended a private normal school for black students for two years. Instead of college preparatory subjects, these normal schools focused on practical skills such as farming or training students to become elementary teachers in all-black schools. One of his teachers at the normal school saw how smart and talented Julian was and helped him enroll at DePauw. Still, Julian had to catch up on his studies by taking high school courses for two years along with his college studies.

Compared with the white students around him, Julian felt "hopelessly" behind. They had taken math and science classes in high school. They were well prepared for college and seemed brilliant to Julian.

Julian was finally able to live on campus after he found a job waiting tables in a fraternity house.

DePauw University was founded by the Methodist Church in 1837.

In winter, he shoveled coal into the house's furnace. The fraternity allowed him to live in an unused room. Sometimes he also earned money by digging ditches. All the while he studied both high school and college courses. Often he had to stay up long past midnight to get his schoolwork done. His hard work paid off. After two years, he had caught up with his classmates.

Julian's dream was to become a chemist. At first Julian's father wanted his son to become a doctor. There was great need in the black community for physicians, and James Julian feared there was little opportunity in the world for black chemists. However, a black role model had appeared about the time Julian went to college. A determined young African-American named St. Elmo Brady succeeded in getting a doctorate from the University of Illinois in 1916. He became the first African-American in the United States to earn a doctorate in chemistry. Julian convinced his father that if Brady could do it, so could he.

> *To some people, "organic" means growing fruits and vegetables without the use of chemical fertilizers or pesticides. To scientists, it has a different meaning. It refers to a type of chemistry involving compounds that contain carbon atoms.*

At DePauw, Julian took all the chemistry courses that he could. His favorite was organic chemistry—the chemistry of living things and things that were once alive. What makes organic compounds special is that they all contain carbon atoms.

By the time Julian went to college, scientists still had a great deal to learn about organic compounds. They knew that carbon atoms bond, or stick, to one another. They knew carbon atoms can form long chains and rings of five or six carbon atoms. Models that scientists made of these carbon chains and rings looked like balls and sticks. The carbon chains and rings stick together in various patterns. The patterns form the various kinds of organic molecules.

Julian (top left) was the only African-American in the DePauw University Chemistry Club.

35 ⁕

Julian spent much of his spare time in the laboratory doing experiments. He received a great deal of encouragement from chemistry professor William Blanchard. Through hard work, Julian did more than just catch up to his white classmates. His grades soared. When he graduated in 1920, he was at the top of his class. His proud family gathered to see Julian graduate. He also graduated as a member of the Phi Beta Kappa society. Only the top-ranked students of a college or university, usually juniors or seniors, are invited to become members of this academic society.

Julian's great-grandmother was there. She did something that touched him very deeply. He said:

Percy Julian graduated as the valedictorian of his class.

At commencement time, my great-grandmother bared her shoulders, and she showed me, for the first time, the deep scars that had remained from a beating she had received when, one day, during the waning days of the Civil War, she went through the Negro quarters and cried out, "Get yourselves ready, children. The Yankees are coming. The Lord has heard our prayers!" And then, proudly, she took my Phi Beta Kappa key in her hand and said, "This is worth all the scars."

James and Elizabeth Julian were so pleased with Julian's success at DePauw that they moved the whole family to Greencastle. Eventually all the Julian children graduated from DePauw. His two brothers went on to become physicians and his three sisters went on to earn master's degrees.

Meanwhile, Julian faced more racial discrimination. Most of his classmates were accepted to graduate schools where they could work on master's degrees and doctorates. Julian did not receive a response to his applications to graduate school. He recalled:

I shall never forget a week of anxious waiting in 1920 to see if I could get into graduate school. I had worked hard for four years. I stood by as day by day my fellow students in chemistry came by saying ... "I am going to Ohio State," ... "I am going to Yale," ... "Where are you going?" ... and they answered for me, "You must be getting the Harvard plum." I could stand the suspense no longer. I went to Professor Blanchard ... and he showed me numerous letters from men who had really meant "god" to me, great American chemists of their day. "I'd advise you to discourage your bright colored lad," they wrote. "We couldn't get him a job when he's done, and it'll only mean frustration. … Why don't you find him a teaching job in a Negro college in the South? He doesn't need a Ph.D. for that."

Julian decided to face the facts. There were no positions for an African-American chemist. He would be better off teaching at one of the all-black universities in the South, as the white college professors advised.

Some of the schools set up after the Civil War to teach former slaves how to read and write became all-black colleges and universities. They were operated by religious organizations based in the North. The most famous of these schools were Fisk University in Nashville, Tennessee, and Howard University in Washington, D.C. Not knowing what else to do, Julian went back to the South. He took a job teaching chemistry at Fisk.

In his heart, Julian kept alive the hope of continuing his education as a chemist. With the help of his former professor, Blanchard, he won a scholarship to Harvard University. In 1923, he earned his master's degree in chemistry and hoped to stay on at Harvard for a doctorate. Racial discrimination, however, proved again to be an obstacle. People working on doctorates usually support themselves by working as

Howard University was founded in 1867 and named after Civil War hero General Oliver Howard.

teaching assistants. At that time, however, Harvard would not allow an African-American to teach white students. After doing research for three years at Harvard, Julian took a job teaching chemistry at a black college in West Virginia.

In 1928, after two years in West Virginia, he moved to Howard University to take over as chair of the chemistry department. He replaced his hero, St. Elmo Brady, who took a job at Fisk. Julian set about improving Howard's chemistry program and created a million-dollar chemistry laboratory. Just one year later, Julian had the opportunity he had longed for—a chance to earn a doctorate. ஒ

4 THE VIENNA EXPERIENCE

Chapter

෨෨෨

In 1929, Percy Julian took a leave of absence from Howard University and set sail for Europe. His goal was to earn his doctorate in Austria. At that time, only about 60 black people in the United States had earned doctoral degrees. Julian's journey to Europe was made possible by a fellowship—a sum of money given to scholars or scientists that allows them to do further studies—from the Rockefeller Foundation. Julian decided he wanted to earn a doctorate by studying with a great German chemist, Ernst Späth, at the University of Vienna in Austria.

Like Julian, Späth was interested in natural products chemistry, which focuses on chemicals made by plants. Scientists and doctors had long known that plant chemicals could affect people. The ancient

Percy Julian traveled to Vienna, Austria, to earn a Ph.D. in chemistry.

The University of Vienna is one of the largest universities in central Europe.

Greeks, for example, discovered that the bark and leaves of the willow tree could ease pain. Since the late 1700s doctors had treated heart problems with the leaves of the foxglove plant. What was it in these plants that could be powerful medicines? In the early 1900s, the most exciting branch of chemistry was natural products chemistry. Natural products researchers wanted to know what was in the "chemical labs" of the plants.

Organic chemists found that some plants made powerful compounds called alkaloids. They found that alkaloids are made of carbon rings. The rings are attached to each other in many ways. In addition, an alkaloid molecule contains at least one nitrogen atom.

Späth had two goals as he studied alkaloids. First,

he wanted to find the chemicals that make up an alkaloid. Next, he wanted to synthesize the alkaloid—make it in the laboratory from its chemical parts.

While in West Virginia and at Howard University, Julian had read about Späth's work in scientific journals. He learned that Späth had obtained two alkaloids. He had isolated pure caffeine from coffee beans. Caffeine is the plant chemical that makes people feel awake and alert after drinking coffee. He also isolated nicotine from tobacco leaves. Then Späth learned what makes up the chemical parts of caffeine and nicotine. Finally he mixed the chemical parts together to make synthetic caffeine and nicotine in the laboratory.

In his labs in West Virginia and then at Howard University, Julian worked on repeating Späth's experiments. A scientist's ability to repeat another's work is very important. Being able to repeat an experiment several times with the same outcome proves that the results are correct. Julian admired Späth's work so much that he decided to earn his doctorate in Späth's laboratory.

When Julian arrived in Vienna, he entered a far different world than any he had known. Many Europeans had never seen a black person. They were curious about him, but they treated him as an equal. Right away, Julian became popular with his classmates. They liked his intelligence and good humor.

In addition, Julian brought big wooden crates filled with glass tubes, beakers, and other fine lab equipment. There was little good equipment in the labs at the University of Vienna. Austria, like most of Europe, had suffered hard times in the early 1900s. First, a destructive war—World War I—was fought in Europe from 1914 to 1918. Then poverty and hardship began in Austria before the country had recovered from the effects of war. There was not much money for lab equipment, but thanks to Julian, Späth and his students now had the best-equipped chemistry lab in the university.

Julian fit right into the social life of Vienna, too. He learned to speak German quite well. He became good friends with another student, Edwin Mosettig. Edwin brought him home and made him part of the Mosettig family. Frau Mosettig, his mother, was a musician. She taught Julian to play the piano. With the Mosettig family, Julian went to the Vienna Opera. He swam in the Danube River, played tennis, and tried skiing. Julian became good friends with another student, Joseph Pikl. Joseph would play an important role in Julian's later work. Julian entertained Pikl, the Mosettigs, and other friends at a fine apartment he had rented, a short walk from the laboratory.

Despite all the fun he had, Julian was in Vienna to work. He was at Späth's laboratory every morning before 8 A.M. Pikl said:

In the laboratory ... he was particularly noted for his neatness ... the cleanliness of his workbench, his ready and contagious laugh, completely uninhibited. All the 15 other graduate students in the room were his friends.

Before leaving Austria, Julian visited the daughters of a chemist he had befriended in Vienna.

Späth gave Julian a difficult chemical task to work on for his doctorate. Julian's task was to identify and analyze alkaloids in a plant that grew wild in the woods around Vienna. The plant contained compounds that could treat pain and irregular heartbeats. He had to figure out what molecules the compound contained and how the molecules were arranged. Julian spent long hours grinding up the plant's seeds, dissolving them in liquids, and separating out compounds. Finally Julian succeeded and was awarded a doctorate in 1931. He also succeeded in making a great impression on Späth, who was known as a tough and demanding teacher. "An extraordinary student," said Späth, "his like I have not seen before in my career as a teacher."

The years Julian spent in Vienna were significant not only to his career. They had "great influence in developing the personality of Julian," recalled Pikl. "For the first time in his life, he was completely at ease, no open or hidden barriers, really an equal among equals."

Julian claimed those years were among the best he had ever known. However, once he had his doctorate, it was time to return home to the United States and Howard University. When Julian set sail across the Atlantic Ocean, he took Pikl along with him. Together, they went to work at Howard. Julian returned to his job as chair of Howard's chemistry department.

Julian wanted not only to teach, but also to continue doing important chemical research. He was determined to make the chemistry laboratory at Howard a first-class research lab. His plans, however, did not work out. Before long, Julian became involved in a complicated situation at Howard. He had conflicts with some of the faculty members. The disputes affected Julian's ability to be an effective department

A chemistry lab at Howard University in the early 1900s

head, and so within a year of earning his doctorate, Julian resigned. He had no job, and there were few jobs for anyone because the Great Depression had taken hold in the United States. As a black chemist, he had no idea who would hire him. His career seemed to be in ruins.

Then in 1932, his old friend and mentor, William Blanchard, stepped in. Blanchard suggested that Julian return to DePauw. He would not be a professor, but he would teach chemistry labs. With no other options, Julian accepted and took his friend Pikl with him. Little did Julian know that he was on the verge of a discovery that would make him known to scientists all over the world. ✍

Chapter

5 THE FIRST GREAT TRIUMPH

❧⟨∞⟩❧

"It all began with a simple little bean," Percy Julian liked to say, "the Calabar bean. It was a beautiful, purple bean when I first got it. But it is not only beautiful in its appearance, but also in the laboratory it has within it."

Julian had been working enthusiastically with his students at DePauw. He even helped them publish papers describing their lab experiments. He was a very good teacher who made an impression in the classroom. "He put on a grand show," recalled one of his chemistry students. "He would come into his lectures, in his white lab jacket, with a flourish." He also had a dramatic way of speaking to those who attended his labs. "He was oratorical in a way some great scientist from London or Berlin might be."

Julian had more time to spend in the chemistry labs as a research fellow at DePauw University.

Julian, however, knew that his career at DePauw was going nowhere. As an African-American, he knew that the university would never let him become a chemistry professor. Yet he still dreamed of making his mark in the world as a chemist. "I decided I had to do things that would make people take more notice of me," he said. With Pikl, he began to work on the difficult task of synthesizing the drug used to treat glaucoma, an eye disease.

Glaucoma is a condition that is more likely to affect people over the age of 40.

Glaucoma is a complicated disease. The fluid inside the eyeball begins to increase. This fluid puts pressure on the optic nerve, which carries signals from the eye to the brain. Unless it is treated, the pressure

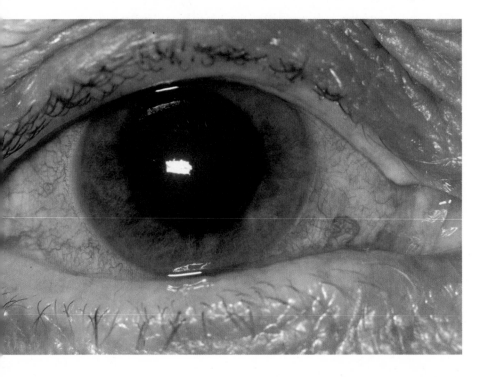

can destroy the optic nerve and cause blindness.

Doctors since the mid-1800s had a way to treat glaucoma. They used a compound with a difficult name—physostigmine. It was another powerful alkaloid from a plant. Physostigmine came from the Calabar bean, originally grown in Africa. However, natural physostigmine was expensive. Only wealthy people could afford this treatment for glaucoma. Doctors needed a less expensive alternative—synthetic physostigmine.

Synthetic physostigmine would be identical to natural physostigmine. The only difference would be where the two were made. In this case, the natural chemical was made in the Calabar bean. The synthetic one would be made by chemists in a laboratory.

Julian was working on the wild frontier of science. No one had ever synthesized a chemical this complicated. Julian knew that the creation of this compound would mark a great milestone in chemistry.

He and Pikl worked together on the task as they had on all their other research projects. Pikl recalled:

> *We were a good team. Percy generated ideas faster than half a dozen people could critically review and test them. He also did most of the writing, did practically all of the analytical work ... and helped with much of the dish-washing chores.*

The chemicals within Calabar beans have also been used as muscle relaxants.

Julian was not the only one who wanted to tap into the bean's chemical laboratory. A well-known chemist named Sir Robert Robinson at Oxford University in England was also trying to synthesize physostigmine. He wrote several articles explaining his work. Scientists tell others about the experiments they are doing by writing papers in scientific journals. Then other scientists try to repeat the experiments to be sure they are correct. Julian read the papers that Robinson wrote and also did experiments. He decided that Robinson was on the wrong track and was not going to find the simplest way of synthesizing physostigmine.

The race was on to see who would synthesize physostigmine first. Julian and Pikl worked day and night. They heated chemicals. They added oxygen atoms. They took oxygen away. They put mixtures under high pressures. Every time they thought they had figured out one of the steps, they had to test their molecules.

They burned each substance in a glass tube, and the molecules separated into hydrogen, oxygen, carbon, and nitrogen. Then they collected each gas in its own tube and weighed them. Weighing the gases told them how much of each element was in their sample. The trick was to find exactly the right amounts of chemicals to mix together. Also, they had to figure out the exact steps needed to build the compound from its simpler parts. Then one day in 1935, Julian and Pikl believed they had it.

Just as they were getting

Robert Robinson (1886–1975)

Sometimes scientists make a great discovery at almost the same time. For example, three people claimed to have discovered oxygen: amateur English scientist Joseph Priestley, French chemist Antoine Lavoisier, and Swedish chemist Carl Wilhelm Scheele. Priestley discovered oxygen in 1774, but he did not know what it was. He told Lavoisier of his discovery. Lavoisier correctly identified the mysterious gas as oxygen, the substance in air that allows things to burn. Scheele independently identified oxygen in 1777 and called it fire air.

ready to tell the world about their success, Robinson published first. "The shock was almost unbearable," recalled Julian. "We were not the first, just the 'me toos.' Why did he, of so much fame, who didn't at all need the glory, have to snatch the prize from us?"

All was not lost. Julian recalled, "Suddenly, my eye caught something." He noticed the melting point of Robinson's substance. Julian's compound melted at body temperature. The paper stated that Robinson's compound melted at 50 degrees higher. "He hasn't got it!" Julian cried.

Julian published a daring statement: "We believe that the English authors are in error," he stated. Julian's friends, including Pikl, thought that stating this so boldly was a terrible idea. Robinson was one of the world's giants in plant chemistry. If Julian challenged him, and if Julian was wrong, that would be the end of Julian's career. Pikl feared it might be the end of his career, too, because he was helping Julian.

Julian published it anyway. He said:

> *It hit like a bombshell. Telegrams came in from all over the world. My old professor [from] Harvard … wrote: "I pray that you are right. If not, the future may be dark for you."*

Julian and Pikl had to prove they were right. The melting point would determine who was right. Julian and Pikl took two samples. One was natural physostigmine from the Calabar bean. The other was what they hoped was physostigmine made in their laboratory.

If the sample they made really was physostigmine, it would melt at the same temperature as the natural physostigmine. They heated both samples at the same time. Both melted at exactly the same temperature. They had won a great race of science.

While the race was on, Julian was getting ready for his wedding. He had met and fallen in love with a brilliant young woman, Anna Roselle Johnson. Born in Baltimore, Maryland, she would become the first African-American woman in the United States to receive a doctorate in sociology.

On Christmas Eve 1935, he and Anna married. At that point, Anna was still working on her doctorate. After the wedding, she went back to school at the University of Pennsylvania in Philadelphia, and Julian went in search of a good, steady job.

After synthesizing physostigmine, he should have been able to choose from many positions in universities and in industry. Making the drug was a great accomplishment. No one had ever made such a complicated drug in a laboratory. Chemists saw it as one of the most important developments in natural products chemistry.

Eventually the American Chemical Society recognized his accomplishment as one of the official milestones of chemistry. Blanchard wanted DePauw to make Julian the first black professor in a white university. But it didn't happen. Even with

his world famous accomplishment, Julian's race held him back. Few places in the 1930s would hire a black chemist—even a well-known one. ✑

In 1924, President Calvin Coolidge (center, holding hat) posed with members of the American Chemical Society in Washington, D.C.

6 SOYBEAN SCIENTIST

Percy Julian applied for job after job at one university after another. They all turned him down, and no one was ashamed to say they turned him down because he was black. The 1930s was a time of open racial discrimination. Some people even claimed there was a "scientific" basis for racism. They claimed that African-Americans were not intelligent enough to be scientists.

Unable to find a job at a university, Julian tried industry. The outlook seemed hopeful when Dupont Chemical Company invited him and Pikl for a job interview. The Dupont executives offered Pikl a job, but they offered Julian only an apology. "We didn't know you were a Negro," they said.

Julian urged Pikl to take the Dupont job. All jobs

Julian was able to continue his research as director of the Glidden Company's soybean laboratory.

One of Dupont's factories focused on the production of nylon from plant products.

were hard to find during the Great Depression. Pikl went to work for Dupont, and Julian went on with his job search, going from one company to another. "Day by day, as I entered these firms, presented my credentials and asked for a job, the answer almost seemed like it had been transmitted by wire from one firm to the other," he said. "It ran like this: 'We've never hired a Negro research chemist before. We don't know how it would work out.'"

At this point in his job search, Julian considered taking a job as a research chemist at the Institute of Paper Chemistry in Appleton, Wisconsin. Julian was well known at the institute. Some of his former students worked there.

Julian's friends at the institute offered him a job in Appleton. He said:

> *I'd sent many of my students from DePauw to the Institute of Paper Chemistry at Appleton for their doctorate degrees, and I'd become quite well acquainted with the institute, which trained specialists in paper chemistry. And the institute had decided to take pity on a young fellow who really should have [the] opportunity to earn a little bit more money so he could get married and start life, to offer me a job in research.*

They settled many details, including the projects he would start work on. Then someone discovered a major problem. Appleton had a law forbidding African-Americans to stay overnight in the town. The institute might offer Julian a job, but he would not be able to live there.

The members of the institute held an emergency meeting to

Chemistry is important in making paper. Chemists add substances to create papers of various qualities. For example, they add substances called sizings to make paper smooth and shiny. Sizings can control the amount of ink a sheet of paper absorbs. The smoother and shinier the paper is, the less ink it absorbs. Paper for printing photos from a home printer, for example, is very shiny and absorbs little ink. The less ink the paper absorbs, the sharper the picture will be. Unsized paper, such as paper toweling, absorbs lots of liquid. Being absorbent makes paper towels good for mopping up spills. Chemists are always looking for new materials they can use in making paper.

discuss what to do. One of the men attending the meeting was William J. O'Brien, vice president of the Glidden Company. Glidden was building a new plant and research lab in Chicago. O'Brien knew that talent and intelligence had nothing to do with skin color. Julian was a brilliant chemist, and O'Brien decided that he wanted Julian to head the new lab. He offered him a job. Julian sent a telegram with the news to his wife: "Am considering offer Glidden Company in research at $5,000." She replied, "What do you mean 'considering'?"

Chemical research was key to the continued growth of the Glidden Company. The company had started in 1875 as a local maker of varnishes in Ohio. In 1917, a businessman named Adrian D. Joyce bought the company and expanded its product line to include paints, varnishes, and coatings for paper. In 1929, Joyce added E.R. Durkee & Company to make cooking oils and other food products. Joyce was fascinated with soybeans. He believed that soybean processing could become a major new business for Glidden. The new plant and lab in Chicago were built for Glidden's soybean business.

In 1936, Julian moved to Chicago and became director of research for Glidden's new Soya Division. He made history as the first African-American director of any research lab. Julian entered a different kind of research world. In universities, Julian could work on

Julian helped Glidden advance as a chemical business with his research.

just about anything that interested him. Sometimes he did pure research just to find out how a chemical was put together. Sometimes he did research to solve a problem, such as making a synthetic drug for glaucoma. In industry, however, all of his research had to be practical, to solve a problem. He had to work on projects that were of interest to the Glidden Company. His job was to find ways to make Glidden products better. He also had to find new products that Glidden could manufacture and sell. "And so I came to Chicago," he said, "and started in on another fascinating plant, the soybean."

By 1936, soybeans were the new glamour plant. Industries had been interested in soybeans since the early 1900s. Henry Ford gave a big push to using soybeans when he began looking for ways to use farm products in building cars. In the early 1900s, Ford created one of the greatest manufacturing companies in the world, the Ford Motor Company. He also revolutionized industry by developing the assembly line. Cars made on assembly lines were so inexpensive that an ordinary worker could afford to buy one.

Soybeans became widely popular in chemical research in the 1930s.

He continued to look for ways to improve the automobile industry. Ford said:

> I believe that industry and Agriculture are natural partners. Agriculture suffers from lack of a market for its product. Industry suffers from a lack of employment for its surplus men. Bringing them together heals the ailments of both. I see the time coming when a farmer not only will raise raw materials for industry, but will do the initial processing on his farm. He will stand on both his feet— one foot on soil for his livelihood; the other in industry for the cash he needs. Thus he will have a double security. That is what I'm working for!

Soybeans are a blockbuster crop in the United States. Farmers grow more than 3 billion bushels every year. The harvested soybeans are made into many kinds of foods, including soy burgers, soy cheese, soy milk, and even soy ice cream. Some of the crop is used in industry to make glues, plastics, paint removers, lubricating oils, and candles.

Ford bought land to grow soybeans in Michigan. After the soybeans were harvested, they were ground up and separated into soybean oil and soybean meal. Ford set up a research laboratory to see what products could be made from soy oil and meal. From oil, he made paints for his cars. From meal, he made plastics for steering wheels and gearshift knobs.

Following Ford's success, the Glidden Company also decided to look into ways of using soybeans in its manufacturing plants. Julian's first assignment was to find a way of making huge amounts of soy protein for sale and use in Glidden products. Proteins are organic molecules. All cells and tissues are made of protein. Protein can be found in animal products, such as meat and milk. Plant cells and tissues, however, also contain protein.

Glidden wanted to use soy protein in making paper coatings and sizings. At the time, paper companies used a coating called casein, which comes from milk. Julian was able to create the first bulk-volume vegetable protein. Julian's soy protein was much cheaper than casein. Glidden also used the soy protein to make water-based, latex paint. Soy protein sales earned Glidden a great deal of money.

No longer just a researcher, Julian directed more than 30 employees in his laboratory. He oversaw the work of other chemists. He met with engineers about how to build factories for making the products that came from his lab. He also met with executives about the business of making chemicals.

"He was brilliant," said Helen Printy, one of his lab employees. "He would set out a research project, and he would write the introduction and the description of the work, and a conclusion. He did everything except do the experiment."

Out of Julian's lab came an incredible variety of new products from soybeans, including salad dress-

Julian monitored the equipment at Glidden's paint and varnish plant.

ings, smoother chocolate, and pet foods for Glidden's Durkee Foods division. Eventually he made plastics and glues from soy oil and protein. He also produced firefighting foam called Aero-Foam. It was a lifesaver during World War II. In sea battles, ships struck by bombs, missiles, and bullets often caught on fire. Many of these fires were fed by oil from the fuel tanks. Aero-Foam, when sprayed on the fire, suffocated the flames. The foam kept the oil fires from getting the oxygen they needed to burn. The U.S. Navy called it "bean soup." Julian's bean soup saved the lives of many sailors.

Thanks to Julian's efforts, the Soya Division grew rapidly. It eventually became the most profitable division of the Glidden Company. ஒ

7 A WONDERFUL ACCIDENT

⤸⟋⟍⤸

Percy Julian worked in a first-floor office at the Glidden Company Soya Division. His desk was usually piled high with papers. His secretary complained that his desk always looked like it had been hit by a "Kansas windstorm." When the window was open, an unpleasant smell often drifted into the office from the nearby factory where soybeans were being processed.

One day in late 1939 or early 1940, the phone on Julian's desk rang, and a voice on the other end had an urgent message. There had been an accident at Soybean Oil Tank Number 1. Water had leaked into the tank and the oil had been spoiled. "The tank," said the worker, "contains a mass of white solid."

"Now, you understand, this tank contained

Soybeans were the focus of Julian's research as director of the Soya Division at Glidden.

100,000 gallons of refined soybean oil bound for the Durkee Famous Foods plant," said Julian. "If it were ruined, Glidden would be out $200,000. And such a blunder might cost me my job, so I was over there in a jiffy."

When Julian saw the white solids, however, he was not shocked or upset. He was curious and excited. He had seen this kind of thing before. When he had experimented with Calabar beans at DePauw, he had set a dish of the bean oil aside. After a few days, Julian had looked at the oil and saw tiny white solids called crystals in the bottom of the dish. He had analyzed the crystals in his DePauw laboratory and discovered that they were a type of organic chemical called a steroid. This particular steroid was called stigmasterol. How had they formed in the dish of oil? Until the accident with Oil Tank Number 1, he had forgotten about that earlier "accident." He had become too busy with his new job at Glidden to think about it.

The accident in Oil Tank Number 1, however, set off a whirl of thoughts in Julian's mind. It brought together many strands of research that recently had begun to interest him. For example, he had become fascinated with a human female hormone called progesterone, discovered in 1934. Hormones are powerful chemicals that are important to many body functions such as sexual maturity, physical growth, and childbirth. Medical researchers had discovered that progesterone could help women having difficulty with childbirth. It was nicknamed the "pregnancy hormone" because it could prevent some miscarriages. Progesterone was expensive, however. Only tiny amounts could be made from animal parts and products.

Like all hormones, progesterone is a steroid. Medical scientists were learning that the body produces dozens of different steroids. All these steroids have different effects. At the same time, chemists discovered that all steroid molecules are almost alike. They all have a framework made up of the same number of carbon and hydrogen atoms. The framework always contains four carbon rings. Other molecules attached to the framework make each steroid behave differently. It is like a basic bicycle framework. Adding different gears, seats, tires, and handlebars could make a mountain bike, racing bike, or road bike. Even more exciting to Julian was the fact that plants produce steroids. He knew this from the time he had found stigmasterol in his dish of soybean oil.

All of this occurred at a time when Julian was beginning to feel restless. "I was itching to get away from dog foods, paint and oleomargarine, and to tackle nature again with more exacting methods," he recalled.

Julian realized that finding an inexpensive way to make large quantities of progesterone and other steroids from plants could revolutionize medicine. As with physostigmine, he was not the only researcher with this idea. In 1938, chemist Russell E. Marker at Penn State University created progesterone from steroids in sarsaparilla root. Progesterone made from this root, however, was still too expensive.

This was one scientific race that Julian held little hope of winning. German scientists had discovered how to convert stigmasterol to progesterone. The soybean oil produced by Glidden was full of stigmasterol. However, Julian did not know how to extract the stigmasterol. His duties as the lab director at Glidden left little time for such a project.

As Julian studied the "spoiled" soybean oil and thought about the crystals in his dish of oil long ago, he came to a wonderful conclusion. He knew what had separated stigmasterol from the soybean oil: plain water. Adding a little water caused the stigmasterol to form crystals. The crystals fell like snow to the bottom of the tank. The rest of the oil was just fine.

Julian (right) worked with a former student, Arthur Magnani, at the Glidden plant.

> *Electric current, the technical wonder that powers much of modern life, was another accidental discovery. In 1786, an Italian anatomy professor named Luigi Galvani was using a steel scalpel to dissect a frog in his lab. Nearby, his assistant generated a spark from a machine that made static electricity. The spark jumped to the steel scalpel and sent an electric current through the frog. The dead frog's leg began to twitch and jump. It took many years for scientists to figure out that a completed electric circuit caused the twitching. The current flowing through the circuit gave the dead frog an electric shock. Galvanize, a verb that means to shock into action, comes from Galvani's name.*

Julian said:

> *And it was this little accidental discovery—the kind that characterize the development of science so often—that led to a practical method for the isolation of steroids from soybean oil.*

Julian and his researchers quickly developed a process for collecting large amounts of stigmasterol from soybean oil and converting it to progesterone. One day in 1940, an armored car pulled up to Julian's laboratory. Armed guards carried out a 1-pound (0.45-kilogram) package of the hormone worth about $70,000. They delivered it to the Upjohn Company, a pharmaceutical maker in Kalamazoo, Michigan.

In no time, Glidden became a major producer of hormones. After progesterone came the male hormone testosterone and other synthetic sex hormones. Doctors were now able to treat many diseases caused by a person not having

Cortisone tablets were made on a production line at the Upjohn Company.

enough of a hormone. They also used the hormones to treat certain cancers. In addition, the sex hormones were used to make birth control pills.

The work of Julian and Marker brought about a revolution in medicine. Finding a way to produce hormones in bulk would have been a great achievement for any chemist's career. However, Julian was about to undertake his greatest work. ✍

8 THE CORTISONE STORY

"Every problem grows into a new problem," Percy Julian would say, "and every new product lays the basis for the manufacture of another new product." This statement was about to be proven true once again. While Julian was in Chicago learning how to mass-produce sex hormones, other exciting steroid research was going on in Rochester, Minnesota. Medical researchers at the Mayo Clinic had discovered a treatment that helped people suffering from rheumatoid arthritis.

The painful disease attacks the joints and cripples people by destroying knee, hip, and elbow joints. It can twist and deform fingers. It can attack the neck and spine. Rheumatoid arthritis has been a problem since ancient times. Archaeologists have found evidence that people suffered from the disease in ancient Egypt, for example. Since ancient times, healers have searched for a cure. No one, however, had found a treatment that worked.

At the Mayo Clinic, Dr. Philip Hench specialized in treating arthritis. In the late 1930s, he began to notice something odd in some of his patients. Sometimes their arthritis symptoms suddenly improved. These patients had suffered a type of liver problem, were pregnant, or had undergone surgery. Did their bodies produce some type of natural drug? He called this mysterious natural drug Substance X.

At the same time, in a laboratory at the Mayo Clinic, researcher Edward Kendall found hormones made by tiny glands above the kidneys. They are called adrenal glands. He found a total of six hormones and named them Compounds A through F. Hench learned about Kendall's discovery. He began to wonder if one of the hormones might be Substance X. The two men studied what was known about the hormones. They decided that Substance X might be the hormone named Compound E, which came to be called cortisone.

In 1941, Hench decided to try injecting cortisone into an arthritis patient. There was a big problem, however. Hench did not have enough of the hormone for a test. Researchers at Merck & Company worked for years to synthesize enough doses for a trial. In

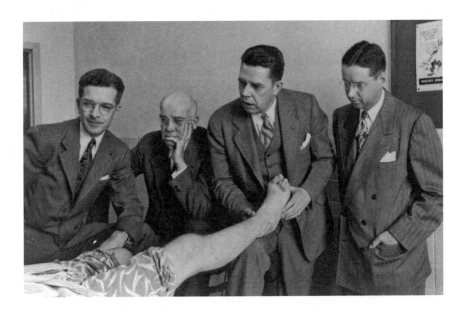

Doctors Charles Slocumb (from left), Edward Kendall, Philip Hench, and Howard Polley of the Mayo Clinic tested the effects of cortisone on a patient with arthritis.

1948, Hench and a team of Mayo doctors were finally able to inject cortisone into a patient. Three days later, the patient had greatly improved. Hench tried cortisone on a total of 14 patients. The hormone seemed like a miracle cure. The news flashed around the world. Thousands of people with rheumatoid arthritis begged for cortisone treatments.

The cortisone Hench used came from oxen, and he had only a few grams. It would take thousands of animals to provide enough cortisone to treat even one patient for one year. A better way of producing cortisone was needed. Chemists in laboratories all over the world went to work on finding a better way of synthesizing cortisone. The race was on, and Julian was in it.

Cortisone is a steroid. It has the same carbon framework as all other steroids. Julian believed that he could make cortisone from soybeans just as he made other steroids. So he began by making a compound similar to cortisone. He called it Compound S. His plan was to then convert Compound S to cortisone. He knew that Compound S was the same chemical as cortisone except for one oxygen atom. All he had to do was insert that oxygen atom. There was a trick, however. The oxygen atom had to go into one particular place on the steroid molecule.

For two years, Julian and chemists all over the world struggled to insert that one oxygen atom correctly. In 1951, teams of chemists at several other corporations announced success. They had found a way to make cortisone. However, it was still a complicated, expensive way to make the hormone. It looked like Julian had lost this race. It looked like Compound S would not play a role in the development of cortisone.

Six months later, the situation

Steroids can be like miracle drugs for certain medical problems, but they can also be dangerous when not used properly. Athletes who used illegal steroids made headlines in recent years. These steroids are similar to the sex hormone testosterone. Some athletes used the drugs to build up muscles and improve their athletic ability. However, these drugs can damage the heart, liver, and other organs. They can even cause death. Athletes who use them risk both their health and their reputation.

changed completely. Researchers at Upjohn found that a microbe—a mold—could insert that oxygen atom into the steroid molecule. Compound S was an ideal material for the mold to work in. Julian knew how to make huge quantities of Compound S.

Upjohn, however, asked another company, Syntex, to supply steroid material for converting into cortisone. Instead of soybeans, Syntex got its steroids from the Mexican yam. Yams are a richer steroid source than soybeans. Julian suggested that Glidden switch to Mexican yams for producing Compound S. The answer was no. Glidden executives had decided

Workers transported Mexican yams out of a jungle, using their shoulders to bear much of the weight.

to get out of the steroid business.

"I begged [the chairman of Glidden] to hold on," said Julian, "we could set up a simple yam processing plant in Mexico, and with Glidden's influence we could soon be masters of the field. But he had other plans for me in paint and varnish chemistry, new paint to prevent icing on airplane propellers, new shortenings that didn't spatter."

Glidden sold the right to make Compound S to other companies. Julian had to train their chemists in how to mass-produce it. Even though Glidden did not continue in the steroid business, Julian got credit for his contribution to making cortisone a widely available treatment. Cortisone had too many side effects for people with arthritis to use it for very long, but cortisone and similar drugs became important short-term treatments for inflammation. Julian said:

> Many well-meaning people have exaggerated my contribution to the chemistry of the cortisone family of drugs," said Julian. "I've even read somewhere that I was 'the discoverer of cortisone.' Not so. But we made a good choice, indeed, in choosing to synthesize Compound S as our first endeavor. Cortisone could now be made from Compound S simply by dumping it into a tank, throwing in a microorganism and fishing out cortisone after the organism has done its work.

Meanwhile, the Julians had a growing family. In 1940, Percy Julian Jr. was born, and in 1944, Faith was born. In 1950, the Julians decided to buy a bigger house in the upscale Chicago suburb of Oak Park, Illinois. At that time few African-Americans lived in the mainly white suburbs. Not everyone in Oak Park welcomed these new neighbors. Even after finding ways to bring help for people suffering from glaucoma, hormone disorders, and severe arthritis, Julian still had to endure racial insults.

During Thanksgiving weekend, just before the Julian family moved in, someone tried to firebomb their new house. "My dad was out of town, and my

Cortisone shots are often used to reduce inflammation around knees and other joints.

mom got a call from the Oak Park Fire Department," recalled Percy Julian Jr. They asked her to come to the house, and she brought the children with her.

Percy Jr. remembered the event well:

> *Even as a 10-year-old I knew that this was arson. There was no attempt to hide this, to make it look like an accident. I see these bottles, these huge bottles, and I could smell gasoline. The stairs were soaked all the way up to the second floor. They lit the fuse on the outside. The door caught on, but it was sealed so well that the flames couldn't get under the door. But had the bottles caught, the flames would have gone right up the stairwell—a natural chimney—and the house could've been a total loss. And I looked at my mom, and I said, "Why would anybody do this?" And she explained it: They didn't want us to live there ... because of the color of our skin.*

Julian had just been named Chicagoan of the Year by the *Chicago Sun-Times*. The newspaper ran an editorial condemning the arsonists for their cowardly attack.

Months went by and there were no further problems. Percy and Anna Julian felt it was safe to travel out of town and leave the children at home in the care of other adults. While they were out of town, they were shocked to read in the newspaper that

someone had thrown a bomb at the Julian house. It exploded under the children's bedroom windows.

Percy Julian with his wife, Anna, and two kids, Percy Jr. and Faith

"My dad was angry when he came home," said Percy Jr. "I mean really angry, and clearly ready to fight. He looked at this as an attempt to murder his kids."

Julian's Oak Park neighbors were also outraged by the attack. They published a signed letter in the *Sun-Times*:

> *We, as citizens of Oak Park, wish to express the dismay and indignation we feel regarding the further attack on the*

sanctity and security of Dr. Julian's home. We ask Dr. Julian and his family to accept our sincere apology that such un-American and bigoted action should occur in our village. ...

Chicago newspapers reported the attack on Julian's family.

GUARD DR. JULIAN'S HOME
Chicagoan Of The Year's House Target Of Vandals

DR. JULIAN'S HOME

The man voted Chicago's outstanding citizen of 1949, Dr. Percy Julian, hired armed guards, Thursday, to protect his home from vandals who soaked the walls with kerosene and hurled firebrands inside the basement, Thanksgiving eve.

Dr. Julian, developer of synthetic arthritis medicines, and world renowned chemist recently purchased the 10-room home in the exclusive Oak Park section. He planned to move his family there in two weeks.

Despte the attempt to burn the

If those who threw the bomb thought they could frighten the Julians into leaving Oak Park, they were wrong. Julian said:

> *Once the violence began, Anna and I felt we had no choice but to stay. To leave would have been cowardly and wrong. The right of a people to live where they want to, without fear, is more important than my science. I was ready to give up my science and my life to bring a halt to this senseless terrorism.*

The Julian family had more support than ever from most residents of Oak Park. This time hundreds of their neighbors gathered outside the Julian home to demonstrate how much they valued and welcomed the Julian family.

Although the Julians continued to receive death threats, there was no more violence. Percy Julian directed his energy to working for more fair housing in Oak Park. By the 2000s, Oak Park would become one of the most diverse and integrated communities in the United States. ❧

Chapter

9 A Lab of His Own

೧◇◇◇೧

During the 1950s, Percy Julian's family life became more settled. His professional life, however, went through a new upheaval. When Glidden got out of the steroid business, Julian wanted to take on different scientific challenges. He was interested in finding new steroids. He was no longer interested in developing new paints and cooking oils. In 1953, he quit his job at Glidden and struck out on his own. He founded Julian Laboratories in Franklin Park, Illinois. He also set up a company in Mexico to make steroids from the Mexican yam. In addition to being a chemist, he had to become a businessman as well. His first job was to create a modern lab.

"We had left the Glidden Company and moved out to this place that was loaded with rats and mice and

Julian paved the way for African-Americans interested in careers in chemistry.

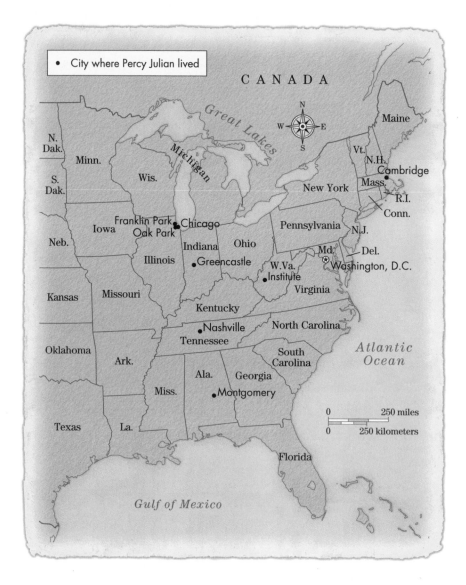

• City where Percy Julian lived

CANADA

Great Lakes

Maine

N. Dak.

Minn.

Michigan

Vt.

N.H.

Cambridge

S. Dak.

Wis.

New York

Mass.

R.I.

Conn.

Iowa

Franklin Park
Oak Park
Chicago

Pennsylvania

N.J.

Neb.

Indiana

Ohio

Md.

Del.

Illinois

Greencastle

W.Va.

Washington, D.C.

Kansas

Missouri

Institute

Virginia

Kentucky

Nashville

North Carolina

Tennessee

Oklahoma

Ark.

South
Carolina

*Atlantic
Ocean*

Ala.

Georgia

Miss.

Montgomery

0   250 miles
0   250 kilometers

Texas

La.

Florida

Gulf of Mexico

Julian resided in several cities throughout the eastern United States, as well as in Vienna, Austria.

everything else," recalled an employee. "You couldn't eat your lunch without a mouse coming out."

They set to work and created a clean, neat lab for producing steroids. Julian's company made substances similar to Compound S. Most of the major U.S. drug companies bought the substances. The drug companies added the finishing touches that turned Julian's compounds into medicines.

As a businessman, Julian's goal was to make money. In time, Julian became a millionaire, but he had other goals, too. He wanted to keep lowering the costs of steroids. He wanted people to be able to afford the drugs. He also was determined to hire African-American chemists. Many young chemists got their start at Julian Laboratories. "I'm proud to say that our laboratories in Franklin Park employed more black chemists than any other facility in America," recalled one of those chemists.

At Glidden and later in his own lab, Julian worked long hours. He was often late for dinner. "Science can be a hard taskmaster," said his wife, Anna. "Dinner can be at seven or 11, as far as the true disciple of chemistry is concerned."

Julian's wife, Anna, was a well-known person aside from her famous husband. After marrying, she was actively involved with many community organizations, serving as a trustee for several schools and educational groups and on government advisory commissions. After Julian established his own business, she served as its vice president and treasurer. She served on the boards of the NAACP Legal Defense and Educational Fund, the United Nations Association, and several other organizations. Anna received many awards for her efforts and three honorary doctorates. She died in Oak Park in 1994 at age 90.

Nevertheless, he took time to work for racial justice. He became active in the National Association for the Advancement of Colored People and the Urban League. He led a major campaign to raise funds for civil rights lawyers.

Rewards and recognition at last came his way. Universities, even those that had refused to hire him in the 1930s, were eager to recognize him in the 1960s and 1970s. He was awarded a total of 18 honorary degrees. He also served on the boards of trustees of several universities and other organizations.

DePauw University recognized its famous graduate by awarding him an honorary doctorate and establishing the Julian Science and Mathematics Center in his honor. A high school in Chicago and a middle school in Oak Park were named for him. In 1947, the NAACP awarded him its Spingarn Medal for distinguished achievement by an African-American. In 1973, he became the second African-American member of the National Academy of Sciences.

In 1961, Julian sold his laboratory to what became the GlaxoSmithKline drug company. He received millions of dollars,

The Spingarn Medal of the NAACP has been awarded to a distinguished African-American every year since 1914. The medal was set up by Joel E. Spingarn, a white NAACP leader and chairman of the board. A teacher of literature at Columbia University in New York City, he encouraged African-American writers.

Julian was the 32nd recipient of the Spingarn Medal.

which allowed him to live comfortably in his retirement. However, he was always involved with plants. He loved to garden. In springtime people stopped to admire the beautiful tulips growing in his Oak Park yard. "The tulips just went on forever," recalled Percy Jr. "My dad, he'd be out there in his black beret, and my sense was that he had this love affair with growing things."

The Decalogue
Society of Lawyers

Award of Merit

FOR THE YEAR, 1950

Presented to

Dr. Percy L. Julian

For Distinguished service to his country
as patriot and scientist, for his outstanding creative achievements in the
interest of the common good, for the boon and
blessings his scientific learning and discoveries
have bestowed upon man, for his unparalleled
devotion to the needs of humanity, the cause
of decency and the progress of free America.

Chicago, Illinois, March 1, 1951

*Julian proudly
displayed
one of his
awards for his
contributions
to science and
medicine.*

Julian lived and grew plants at his Oak Park
home until the 1970s, when he was diagnosed with
liver cancer. Still he tried to go on. "He did not accept
the fact ... that he was going to die. He just seemed
to have other plans," said Risher Watts, who was his

doctor when Julian died of the disease on April 19, 1975, at the age of 76.

The awards and recognition continued. Almost 20 years after his death, the U.S. Postal Service issued a Percy L. Julian commemorative stamp.

It was not just governments, organizations, and universities that thanked Julian for his contributions. He also heard from ordinary people who were helped by his work.

"I definitely was aware that my grandfather was special," said Katherine Julian, a physician. "I remember playing with a doll that had been sent to him by a woman." She also remembered why the woman had sent her grandfather a doll:

> *She had such bad arthritis that she couldn't use her hands. And after using cortisone, she was able to knit this doll and sent it to him. And I remember holding the doll and playing with the doll, and realizing that he had helped her, and that that was something that was really special.*

JULIAN'S LIFE

1899

Born April 11 in Montgomery, Alabama

1916

Becomes a "subfreshman" at DePauw University; works in a fraternity

1920

Graduates from DePauw with bachelor's degree and top honors

1900

1909

The National Association for the Advancement of Colored People (NAACP) is founded

1914

Archduke Franz Ferdinand is assassinated, launching World War I (1914–1918)

1920

American women get the right to vote

WORLD EVENTS

1923

Earns master's
degree from
Harvard University

1926

Teaches chemistry
in West Virginia

1920–1922

Teaches chemistry
at Fisk University

1925

1927

Charles
Lindbergh makes
the first solo non-
stop transatlantic
flight from New
York to Paris

1922

The tomb of
Tutankhamen is
discovered by
British archaeologist
Howard Carter

1923

Irish civil war
ends and the
rebels sign a
peace treaty

Life and Times

JULIAN'S LIFE

1931
Earns doctorate
from the University
of Vienna; briefly
returns to Howard

1932
Takes teaching
and research job
at DePauw

1928
Heads chemistry
department at
Howard University

1930

1930
Clyde Tombaugh
discovers Pluto; he
was 24 years old

1933
Nazi leader Adolf
Hitler is named chan-
cellor of Germany

1928
Walt Disney makes
the first sound
cartoon, *Steamboat
Willie* starring
Mickey Mouse

WORLD EVENTS

1935

Synthesizes physostigmine; marries on Christmas Eve

1936

Becomes head of Glidden's Soya Division in Chicago

1940s

Synthesizes sex hormones and other steroids; invents Aero-Foam, which saves sailors on burning ships

1940

1935

Persia is renamed Iran

1936

African-American athlete Jesse Owens wins four gold medals at the Olympic Games in Berlin in the face of Nazi racial discrimination

1941

Japanese bombers attack Pearl Harbor, Hawaii, on December 7 and the United States enters World War II

JULIAN'S LIFE

1948

Develops a way
to synthesize
cortisone

1950

Named Chicagoan
of the Year; home in
Oak Park, Illinois,
firebombed

1953

Founds Julian
Laboratories

1950

1950

North Korea invades
South Korea, which
begins the Korean War

1948

Milton Berle's variety
show attracts a huge
audience and launches
the television era

1954

In *Brown v. Board
of Education*, the
Supreme Court rules
that deliberate public
school segregation
is illegal

WORLD EVENTS

1960s

Becomes a million-aire from steroid compound sales

1973

Named a member of National Academy of Sciences

1975

Dies April 19 of liver cancer

1975

1963

Martin Luther King Jr. delivers his "I Have a Dream" speech to more than 250,000 people attending the March on Washington

1974

Scientists find that chlorofluorocarbons—chemicals in coolants and propellants—are damaging Earth's ozone layer

1975

Bill Gates and Paul Allen found Microsoft, which will become the world's largest software company

NAME: Percy Lavon Julian

PLACE OF BIRTH: Montgomery, Alabama

DATE OF BIRTH: April 11, 1899

EDUCATION: Bachelor's degree, DePauw University, 1920; master's degree, Harvard University, 1923; doctorate, University of Vienna, 1931

FATHER: James Julian

MOTHER: Elizabeth Julian

SPOUSE: Anna Roselle Johnson (1903–1994)

DATE OF MARRIAGE: December 24, 1935

CHILDREN: Percy Jr. (1940–2008) Faith (1944–)

DATE OF DEATH: April 19, 1975

FURTHER READING

Bial, Raymond. *The Super Soybean*. Morton Grove, Ill.: Albert Whitman & Company, 2007.

Kessler, James H., J.S. Kidd, Renee A. Kidd, and Katherine A. Morin. *Distinguished African American Scientists of the 20th Century*. Phoenix, Ariz.: Oryx Press, 1996.

Louis, Haber. *Black Pioneers of Science and Invention*. San Diego: Odyssey Classics, 2007.

Landau, Elaine. *The Civil Rights Movement in America*. Danbury, Conn.: Children's Press, 2007.

Morrison, Toni. *Remember: The Journey to School Integration*. Boston: Houghton Mifflin, 2004.

LOOK FOR MORE SIGNATURE LIVES BOOKS ABOUT THIS ERA:

Maya Angelou: *Poet, Performer, Activist*

George Washington Carver: *Scientist, Inventor, and Teacher*

Langston Hughes: *The Voice of Harlem*

Wilma Mankiller: *Chief of the Cherokee Nation*

Thurgood Marshall: *Civil Rights Lawyer and Supreme Court Justice*

Annie Oakley: *American Sharpshooter*

Will Rogers: *Cowboy, Comedian, and Commentator*

Nikola Tesla: *Physicist, Inventor, Electrical Engineer*

Alice Walker: *Author and Social Activist*

Booker T. Washington: *Innovative Educator*

ON THE WEB

For more information on this topic,
use FactHound.
1. Go to *www.facthound.com*
2. Choose your grade level.
3. Begin your search.
The book's ID number is 9780756540890
FactHound will find the best
sites for you.

HISTORIC SITES

Percy L. Julian Science and Math Center
DePauw University
602 S. College Ave.
Greencastle, IN 46135
Contains classrooms, laboratories,
department offices, and the Prevo
Science Library

Percy L. Julian Exhibit
West Town Museum of Cultural History
104 S. Fifth Ave.
Maywood, IL 60153
Museum in the western suburbs of
Chicago celebrating the area's black
history and notable African-Americans

alkaloids
nitrogen-containing organic compounds from
plants that have powerful effects on human beings

biogenesis
process of making chemical compounds by
living organisms

cortisone
hormone made by adrenal glands; can also be
made synthetically

freedmen
people who were released from slavery

hormone
substance, often a steroid, that regulates body
processes, such as growth and sexual development

protein
organic compounds found in the cells of all
living things

organic chemistry
study of compounds containing carbon

Reconstruction
period following the Civil War, from 1865 to 1877,
when the federal government governed states
in the former Confederacy and granted rights to
African-Americans

segregated
separated or set apart by race, gender, or religion

synthesize
to make chemical compounds from chemical parts

white supremacist
person who believes that the white race is
superior to all other races

Source Notes

Chapter 1

Page 12, line 2: "Forgotten Genius: Julian Speaks." *PBS*. 6 Feb. 2007. 9 Oct. 2008. www.pbs.org/wgbh/nova/julian/spea-nf.html

Page 14, line 24: Bernhard Witkop. "Biographical Memoirs: Percy Lavon Julian." *The National Academies Press*. 9 Sept. 2008. www.nap.edu/html/biomems/pjulian.html, p. 234.

Chapter 2

Page 17, line 4: Ibid.

Page 26, line 6: "Science Alive: Percy Julian." *Chemical Heritage Foundation*. 9 Oct. 2008. www.chemheritage.org/scialive/julian/activities/1b.html

Page 26, line 20: "Biographical Memoirs: Percy Lavon Julian," p. 234.

Page 29, line 1: Ibid.

Chapter 3

Page 32, line 14: Ibid.

Page 33, line 13: "Forgotten Genius: Transcripts." *PBS*. 6 Feb. 2007. 9 Oct. 2008. www.pbs.org/wgbh/nova/transcripts/3402_julian.html

Page 36, line 23: Ibid.

Page 37, line 18: Louis Haber. *Black Pioneers of Science and Invention*. New York: Harcourt, Brace, Jovanovich, 1970, pp. 125–126.

Chapter 4

Page 45, line 1: "Biographical Memoirs: Percy Lavon Julian," p. 234.

Page 46, line 5: Ibid., p. 233.

Page 46, line 9: Ibid., p. 234.

Chapter 5

Page 49, line 1: "Forgotten Genius: Transcripts."

Page 49, line 10: Ibid.

Page 50, line 5: Ibid.

Page 51, line 23: "Biographical Memoirs: Percy Lavon Julian," p. 235.

Page 54, line 3: "Forgotten Genius: Transcripts."

Page 54, line 10: Ibid.

Page 54, line 19: "Biographical Memoirs: Percy Lavon Julian," p. 235.

Page 55, line 2: "Forgotten Genius: Transcripts."

Chapter 6

Page 59, line 13: Ibid.

Page 60, line 3: Ibid.

Page 61, line 4: "Forgotten Genius: Julian Speaks."

Page 62, line 9: "Forgotten Genius: Transcripts."

Page 63, line 10: Ibid.

Page 65, line 4: "Soy Bean Bulletin From Henry Ford—Henry Ford's Biological Car." *The Edison Institute of Technology*. April 1935. 9 Oct. 2008. www.hbci.com/~wenonah/new/soybean.htm

Page 66, line 22: "Forgotten Genius: Transcripts."

Chapter 7

Page 69, line 5: "Biographical Memoirs: Percy Lavon Julian," p. 239.

Page 69, line 13: "Forgotten Genius: Transcripts."

Page 69, line 15: "Biographical Memoirs: Percy Lavon Julian," p. 237.

Page 72, line 12: "Forgotten Genius: Transcripts."

Page 74, line 2: Ibid.

Chapter 8

Page 77, line 1: *Black Pioneers of Science and Invention*, p. 136.

Page 82, line 2: "Forgotten Genius: Transcripts."

Page 82, line 18: Ibid.

Page 83, line 13: Ibid.

Page 84, line 5: Ibid.

Page 85, line 3: Ibid.

Page 85, line 10: "Letters to the Editor." *Chicago Sun Times*. 3 July 1951.

Page 87, line 4: "Forgotten Genius: Transcripts."

Chapter 9

Page 89, line 14: Ibid.

Page 91, line 16: Ibid.

Page 91, line 24: Ibid.

Page 93, line 5: Ibid.

Page 94, line 3: "Forgotten Genius: Those That Knew Him." *PBS*. 6 Feb. 2007. 9 Oct. 2008. www.pbs.org/wgbh/nova/julian/knew.html

Page 95, line 10: Ibid.

Adams, Russell L. *Great Negroes Past and Present*. Chicago: Afro-Am Publishing Company, 1964.

"Archives of DePauw University and Indiana United Methodism: Percy Lavon Julian '20 Family Papers." Depauw University. 9 Sept. 2008. www.depauw.edu/library/archives/dpuinventories/julian_percy_lavon_family.htm

Carson, Clayborne, and Kris Shepard, eds. *A Call to Conscience: The Landmark Speeches of Dr. Martin Luther King, Jr.* New York: Warner Books, 2001.

"Forgotten Genius: Julian Speaks." *PBS*. 6 Feb. 2007. 9 Oct. 2008. www.pbs.org/wgbh/nova/julian/spea-nf.html

"Forgotten Genius: Those That Knew Him." *PBS*. 6 Feb. 2007. 9 Oct. 2008. www.pbs.org/wgbh/nova/julian/knew.html

"Forgotten Genius: Transcripts." *PBS*. 6 Feb. 2007. 9 Oct. 2008. www.pbs.org/wgbh/nova/transcripts/3402_julian.html

Haber, Louis. *Black Pioneers of Science and Invention*. New York: Harcourt, Brace, Jovanovich, 1970.

Kendall, Edward C. *Cortisone*. New York: Scribner, 1971.

Krapp, Kristine M. *Notable Black American Scientists*. Detroit: Gale Research, 1999.

"Letters to the Editor." *Chicago Sun Times*. 3 July 1951.

Morris, Aldon. *The Origins of the Civil Rights Movement: Black Communities Organizing for Change*. New York: Free Press, 1984.

Packard, Jerrold. *American Nightmare: The History of Jim Crow*. New York: St. Martin's Press, 2002.

"Science Alive: Percy Julian." *Chemical Heritage Foundation*. 9 Oct. 2008. www.chemheritage.org/scialive/julian/activities/1b.html

"Soy Bean Bulletin From Henry Ford—Henry Ford's Biological Car." *The Edison Institute of Technology*. April 1935. 9 Oct. 2008. www.hbci.com/~wenonah/new/soybean.htm

Sluby, Patricia Carter. *The Inventive Spirit of African-Americans: Patented Ingenuity*. Westport, Conn.: Praeger, 2004.

Watts, Steven. *The People's Tycoon: Henry Ford and the American Century*. New York: A.A. Knopf, 2005.

Williams, Juan. *Eyes on the Prize: America's Civil Rights Years, 1954–1965*. New York: Viking, 1987.

Witkop, Bernhard. "Biographical Memoirs: Percy Lavon Julian." *The National Academies Press*. 9 Sept. 2008. www.nap.edu/html/biomems/pjulian.html

Wormley, Stanton L., and L.H. Fenderson, eds. *Many Shades of Black*. New York: William Morrow & Company, 1969.